For Dan
and
Gerre,
All best wishes,
Dom Park

MOON PIE SOUTHERN GOTHIC

POEMS BY DONNA PARK

WITH ARTWORK BY MARILYN WRUCKE

EVERGREEN WOMEN'S PRESS
EVERGREEN, COLORADO

ISBN 09671593-0-X
Library of Congress Catalog Card Number: 99-62431

Cover Art is by Marilyn Wrucke

Cover Design by Donna Gallegos

Published by Evergreen Women's Press
P.O. Box 244
Evergreen, Colorado 80437

ACKNOWLEDGMENTS

The author wishes to thank the editors of the following publications, in which some of the poems in this collection first appeared:

Buffalo Bones
The Charlotte Poetry Review
Cold Mountain Review
Chiron Review
The Denny Poems 1993-94 (Winners of the Billee Murray Denny Poetry Contest)
Grapevine
Kalliope
Parnassus Literary Journal
Wind Chimes

Anthologies: *Her Day Begins Flamingo Pink* and *Seasonings for a Colorado Afternoon*

The poem "Tide Pull" was awarded 1st Prize for Poetry in the 1990 National Writers Association contest, and Honorable Mention in the 1994 Wildwood Poetry Prize Competition.

"Massacre", originally published in *Kalliope*, was later selected first prize winner in a *Chiron Review* contest.

"Autumn Sonata" was selected as one of the "Denny Poems" for 1994.

FOR PETER
and for my sons
Patrick and Brendan

TABLE OF CONTENTS

III. MOON PIE SOUTHERN GOTHIC

I.
DELIVERANCE

<<<<<<<<

Suzanne Remembering

"I am a man whom women do not understand."
-- Eric Satie

My hand on the canvas recalls the coast
of your face, a seethe of forehead,
the salt sea grass of your beard, the wry
earnest mollusk perched atop your head.
I fill in the little crumpled pear
smile, velvet suit the color of rain
and old butter, a black umbrella
in your hand, always.

Once you gave me a necklace of sausages
steeped in oregano and thyme, and said you
loved the way I belched. We sailed
red wooden boats to one another across
a pond in the park, and read *Alice*
in Wonderland ***fortissimo*** for hours. Play
the piece "like a nightingale having a toothache,"
you said. Debt and all the rest
would follow, despite the elegance
of your flabby preludes. What's lost
and what's no longer known? It doesn't matter.
There's rain again and the lonely garbage, broken
bottles rolling down the street, pigeon droppings
and a twist of candle, the greasy ends
of sausages.

Separation

Body and spirit are twins;
only God knows which is which.

They came in the night, Angela,
gardeners all in green, to disentangle
your limbs from those of your sister,
to prune back the withered vines
they said could not grow, leaving exposed
tiny glowing nails like rosebuds
innocent as sunrise.*

Years later you will hold your breath at dusk
and sigh, listening for echoes, finger scars
like thorns on your chest, and wonder why
the color pink seems so strangely suffused
with loneliness.

You will see her everywhere,
even in stories where you were meant
to play the starring role. The Three Bears
are unimpressed by your arrival. Someone
who looks like you passed through just days
before. You can't quite get past the part
about wicked stepsisters who keep
their sibling from the ball, and you know,
somewhere deep inside, that if Hansel
had been your brother, he'd never
have made it home.

Even in the tale of that determined
little engine endlessly chugging
up the mountain, there is scant comfort,
no metaphor but the one you carry with you
always, of a heart like a train
pulling too many boxcars, the heaviest
always cast off--clanging
over hill and cliff, coming
to rest finally, forever after,
in a valley filled with honeysuckle,
dogwood, and sweet wild roses.

**At the time of separation, the surgical team painted
the fingernails of the twin chosen to be saved.*

Guaranteed Passage

"Their destiny is to live beneath the earth...
I compare our children to Romeo and Juliet"
-- *Admira Ismic*
Sarajevo, Bosnia-Herzegovina

A glooming peace this morning with it brings;
The sun for sorrow will not show his head.
Go hence, to have more talk of these sad things;
Some shall be pardon'd and some punished;
For never was a story of more woe
Than this of Juliet and her Romeo.
-- *Shakespeare*

These children of Verona are so like my own,
"Blown here by the winds of war,"
Believing in love, promises of passage, the unknown
Future just across the bridge, and all the sore
Green hopes of youth. When Almira, last shot, crawled to Bosko,
Dropped her head, wrapped arms about his chest,
All the world watched the horror that was Sarajevo:
Two children lying unburied and unblessed.
For five white days each faction parried for the prize
Till six crouched Serbs more weary than brave
Bore them up from the shifting dust and flies
Into the shade and solace of their one shared grave.
Unlike those reconciled houses of Montague and Capulet,
Our soldiers still are fighting, our sons and daughters dying yet.

Sobibor

Those who were there
remember the music of Mendelssohn and Brahms,
the warm smiles of the guards at first
and the jade green forest beyond the fence.

Remember the music of Mendelssohn and Brahms
filling the days as the trains rolled in
and the jade green forest beyond the fence,
green as the memory of freedom?

Filling the days as the trains rolled in
horror replacing hope and dreams no longer
green as the memory of freedom --
Rumors of the showers...

Horror replacing hope and dreams no longer
for the ones who didn't return.
Rumors of the showers:
soft whisper and the hiss of gas.

For the ones who didn't return,
a final wordless tribute before
soft whisper and the hiss of gas:
a silent touch, pain too deep for tears.

The three hundred who escaped will always remember
those who were there,
the long bad dream that was Sobibor,
and the last guard's cold smile

La Mirla Pequeña (the little blackbird)

for Aleszandra Berrelez

i.
The music of her name wouldn't
leave him -- a morning sound
like the memory of bells

chiming in the eaves
of the cathedral of Seville.
He dreamed of her at night,

long dark hair floating
like wings above her shoulders.
In his dream she was always

a blackbird. A blackbird, trusting
the wind and the world, she flew
to a man who would hurt her.

ii.
Into private reflection, the attorney
never admitted words like *innocence*
or *evil, perpetrator or defendant.* Soon

enough would begin the parade,
and the long winding enumeration
of excuses. It was almost time

to haul them out, dust them
off and hope they held: prior
abuse, chemical imbalance,

mental disorder -- all those bright
gaudy banners constructed
of such frayed and flimsy cloth.

iii.
In the end the attorney would do
as he had been trained: he would create
around the man who killed

children a small safe space
of curiosity and reason. He would take
the jurors by the hand, open the trap door

and guide them through the corruption
of the cellar -- the grizzled roots
and skulls of rats, the sodden

eels and crumbling spiders. He would
urge them to touch the raw blister
that was his client's heart, the festering

sores that covered the man's whole
life. The attorney would lead
the jury carefully down one step,

then another, from rage and disgust
down to mild discomfort, descending on
to lurid fascination, perhaps

(if he were really good) to pity.
Yes, he could do it -- it might
be done somehow, but not today,

not when his thoughts
were so distracted, his mind
troubled by visions, his ears

filled with the ringing
of cathedral bells
and the call of blackbirds.

Hallomas 1993 -- Denver, Colorado

for Carl Banks, Jr.

Evil must live with us always,
and the fear of ghosts.

Overhead the sun hangs like a bloody
ball of gauze, unraveling. Pumpkins
squat luridly on their porches, sagging
now, the pansies trampled, the grey-white filaments
of spider webs collapsed in bushes, fluttering.
The ballerinas and the pirates are tucked in
against the morning chill, the vampires
and witches back among their books,
and where he fell, only a small dark
stain -- so slight it might have been only
a smudge of berries caught in the crossfire
of falling leaves.

His mother holds the phone to her ear, waiting
for it to be done. She imagines him lying
on a high table in a white room, splayed
open like a squirrel beneath a hawk's talons.
She knows it is a good thing to do,
the right thing really and what he would have
wanted; still she can't stop thinking
of him there, all his fine and private
parts -- his sleepy, Sunday morning eyes,
his kidneys like giant pintos, his strong good
lungs, all his organs, one after
the other, given up like bags of swiftly
melting chocolate parceled out
to strangers.

Across the city, reporters pluck somber
symbols from his lyrics, ironies
worthy of Othello, surprised
that this tall man-child
walked with bandannaed Fates
at nights and pondered death, conjured
words to hold the fear at bay, forged rhymes
to rein in the smoke and shadows
of the street, and the heart.

Down the block, children sit cross-legged
in a chalk circle, listening. Calm and alert
as pigeons, they peck through the dust
for answers. Discarding high-heeled explanations,
they argue quietly the relative bullet-evading
tactics of lying flat or running sideways.
Someone thinks to ask the children if they
are afraid. Not like Halloween, they agree,
not the sweet shrieking terror of ghosts
and beasts and crawling things -- more like
the neighbor's huge black cat, scary at first,
but then you learn his name and still he remains
a little frightening but soft, warm,
so very familiar.

Deliverance

In the beginning he loved the smooth black
shoes, soft wool at his hips, the neat rectangular shape
of days. Racing through his route in gray and blue
government issue, he was a first class postman,
uniformly esteemed and purposeful.
But as the months stretched
like warm taffy into years, too soon
he learned the things he never wanted
to know -- the names of those
who waited for cards that wouldn't
come, and the look of tax bills, neverending
ads for camps and colleges they couldn't
afford, white blood cell counts
nakedly announced on postcards,
and the pale color of third
notices -- sad pastels
of forgetfulness and failure,
and the letterheads that presaged
imminent loss.

Finally, one Tuesday morning
he looked down at his hands, heard the whisper
of all those thousands of little stamps buzzing like bees
through his fingers, felt the weight of the bag
and the heat of the sun's breath on his back,
and there, at precisely 9:07, he knelt
on the sidewalk and wept, and let duty
softly die.

Just before the marshals stormed
his tiny station, the postman sat in the shade
of his garage, shoulders hunched against cool
concrete, watching stray manila missives waft
to the floor, and thought of the things
he might have given them -- cold pears
on a hot day, azaleas maybe or lilacs,
gingersnaps and whistles, a ball
of twine. He hated the complexity
of words, the damned everlastingness
of them, the way they carried on
into your day and followed at your heels
through the evening like a slavering Doberman,
and what could you ever do
with them when you wanted to be
done, when you needed so desperately
just to sleep?

He laughed at how he must look, like a child
adrift on a white raft, a small man floating
on a sea of dead letters. He knew another
courier would do it, gather up the mail
and send it on. He'd be sent somewhere
else, but he'd never really leave.
He would always be their postman,
enveloped in their stories,
part and parcel of their lives.

Guyasmaja Mandala

"What we do can bless this place, bring peace and non-violence, good karma to the people of Denver."
-- Genzin Dakpa, Tibetan monk
Golden Jangtze monastery

four heads bent
in meditation
floating brown shells
of turtles

primary shock of color
your garden growing
peppers and squash

governor, mayor, politicos
wait, learning
enlightenment's timetable

surrounded by pilgrims
mingled breath
of mantis and jay

Chinese artillery fire
one path from Lhasa
to peace

lessons of the Buddha
renunciation of watch
and pocket

grain by grain
sand, remembering stone
awakens

passing of the Tantras
oceans waiting
within a snowflake

love's perfect design
eaten by the Platte
my mother's ashes

red and yellow robes
sunset
over the Himalayas

from a sliver
of window, swell
of moonrise and stars

Luger at your back
lilac in your hand:
equal opportunities
for wisdom

II.
CLOAKROOM OF THE SACRED HEART

<<<<<<<<

Aerobic Valentine

after Stephen Dunn

I love this place, this moist, noisy
women's gym -- I love its dank
and musty smell, its flowered wallpaper

and the buried beads of salt and sloughed
off skin lurking in the fat cropped fibers
of sky blue carpets. I love the walled

mirrors, and the way everyone tries to stand
behind the star because you look smaller
there, and I love the fans whirling

above us, and the reflected sweat and shiver
of us all in rows. I love Marie who's
the biggest one here, for her flowered red

leotard and chalk-white tights hugging
enormous thighs -- I love the heft
and heart of her, and the soft silk

bow bouncing at the back of her neck.
I love the sinewed grace, the sheen of hair
and skin, the svelte tanned tightness

of the twenty-year old model in the second
row, and I love the timid, first-time
woman in gray sweats in the corner

looking down at her feet. I love the slap
of legs and the clap of hands and the bark
of our instructor endlessly exhorting us toward

pain, and I love the groans
that are our inevitable chorus, just as I
love the occasional blond hiss from the front

of the line, the gasping inhalations, the gift
of second wind, and the accompanying scream
of exaltation. I love the slow turtle dance
and the steaming fog emanating from the Aqua-
cizers just behind the glass, and their bright
mermaid march with plastic milk bottles

bobbing at their sides. I love the ache
of arms resisting weights, the pull and surge
and tremble of muscles coming alive.

I love the lack of hairy-legged
arrogance here and the utter dearth
of maleness. I love the strut and slide

and swing of us all becoming music.
I love our gritted teeth and laughter,
our freckles and wrinkles, the curve and sag

and angle of us, our brave and lovely
bones. I love the sweet wild song at the center
of us. I love how we rock on...

Homework

for Brendan

Dusk hovers over your house.
A pale pink light pushes
in at the window, and you
are the only one watching.
Your brother is lost to you,
chasing coyote riffs down valleys
of his bedroom. Sweet wild chords
lure him. The brown furred snail that was your collie
curls on the rug, oblivious. Your parents
lie asleep in a room filled with birds
and Indians, and your grandfather
bobs over his puzzle like a weary woodpecker,
or some indifferent chicken, halfheartedly scrabbling
for corn.

You are brave and good, and you do
the only thing you know. You pull a chair
to the table, embrace a mountain
of paper and books. Alone, you shape into being
reluctant equations, fragile and elusive
formulae, recalcitrant conjugations. You plumb
the depths of DNA and photosynthesis, persuade
paragraphs to align, coax wandering fragments
into symmetry and order. The light changes.
Ever vigilant, you observe carefully
the boundaries of your personal
geography, this landscape you will remember
all your life. You work while watching
over them, keeping all safe
against time,
and the night.

Hard Lessons

for Patrick

Dearest son,
We have given up much
in order to know you:
our odd unthinking attachment
to grades, foolish notions of firm
purpose, thrift, gainful employment; vain hopes
that your clear ideas of personal
cleanliness might extend someday to the far
reaches of your room; misguided
beliefs that baggy pants need belts,
or that shoes invariably require
socks or laces or soles.

Tall eloquent profane one,
so loud and rude, so easy
in your long bones and low-slung
smile, teach us what you know:
how to drive thirty miles on one 64th
of a tank of gas; how to sneak, unpaying,
into the biggest concert of the year;
how to pull the notes from the bottom
of your toes, up through the sleeping strings
of your guitar; now to shape the rhythms
of wind into your own true words.

Sweet child, you are all the music
the world makes when it thinks
no one's listening.

I Am Your Journal,

your port of entry to the unfathomable depths of your feelings.
I will be the first breath of the letters and stories
and poems that travel to other places.
I speak of possibilities.
Do not let these white pages intimidate you,
nor their emptiness upset you.
I ask only that you be honest with me,
and with yourself.
Bring me your songs and your sadnesses,
your worries, fantasies, and frustrations.
Bring me the hurt that screams inside you,
and the small hope hiding in the corner of your heart.
Bring me the fear knotted at the back of your throat,
and the weariness curled at the center of your body.
Bring me also your joys, those bright kites that soar
on winds of your remembering, and the laughter
tumbling from your lips.
Bring me the anger clenched tightly in your fists,
and bring me the tears that must come--
the healing seas of your eyes.
Do not be afraid--no one, save you, will enter here.
This is a place of fragments, eclectic thoughts, beginnings.
It is a place also of synthesis and connections.
You may choose to share all of these pages, some
of them or none at all,
but begin now.
Bring me the best of yourself, and let me know you,
and as your write you will come to know yourself.
Hear that I exist only to give voice
to the thunderous silences
within you,
and I am waiting...

Blessing Flung into the Face of the Wind

Thank you, Manitou, this day for the air
that hurts me, gray screaming
wind that pelts my face, and the snow
like frayed white ropes lashing into limbs
and trunk. Thank you for the battle
that empowers me to feel again the strength
of calves and biceps, muscles stout
as pines piercing the purple skin
of canyons.

And thank you, Spirit, for words
to acknowledge the sun pulling day
up the mountain to the waiting meadow
and the dark sage hills beyond.
My lungs are burning now --
filled with the hot breath of stars
smothered by clouds, and for this, too,
I give thanks.

Cloakroom of the Sacred Heart

Between cracks of thunder, rain murmured
hurried paternosters on the rooftop. Rusting
bins of dusty chalk and broken candles rattled
on their plywood ledge, and the wounded
grey crucifix above me bled deep
into the wall. Out of this tunneled
purgatory issued a miracle: a small hand
reached toward mine. In the dark
your starched white blouse shone bright
as a blessing.

Imprisonment had been handed down for sins
of water--homesick tears, puddle transgressions,
oxfords soiled before morning prayers. "Don't
cry," you whispered. "They don't matter." We dripped
and laughed, plucked fruit from Sister Mary Catherine's
satchel, held hands, told long, forbidden stories.
A tiny worm of light lay trapped beneath
the door. Brown lunch bags huddled
like fat tree frogs on the bottom shelf,
and in the distance, two black crows
cackled and cawed through catechism
until they flew in among the trees
to claim us back to God.

Years later I would acknowledge grace
and love began that day, gifts eternal
as the memory of your hand
in the darkness, the blessed smell
of wet wool and oranges.

Love by the Book

Thank you, Mother,
for your steadfast belief in me,
for your unwavering assertion,
despite evidence to the contrary,
that I was always brilliant,
beautiful, and perfect.

Thank you, too, for gifts
melting and ephemeral,
for creamsicles shared at dusk
on a school playground, for freckles
and your dark hair, sprinkled
with silver, for a place of sea oats
and sand dunes (where I can still see you
walking), for baseball and Hebrew,
for a hundred thousand books and the words
we shared, and even now, for the sound
of your voice, reading through the darkness.

The Service

Yes, Mother, it was beautiful, but do you think
they understood? Not quite kosher, a hybrid ceremony
most certainly, what with the Shakespeare
and the Taos Pueblo blessing and the selections
from *Phantom of the Opera*. Still perhaps a little
too Hebraic for Aunt Rosalie and Frances, there
being no East Tennessee Baptist equivalent, you know,
for the *chazzan** -- that stark clarity
like moonrise hovering in bare branches,
the cold, calm music of his voice. Pastor Randy
tuning up in the church parking lot before
revival was just not the same.

Harold Lee questioned me afterwards, Mother, about
members of the congregation wearing the *tefellin**.
"What were those damn little boxes they had strapped
to their foreheads?" he asked. We should have known
that might present a problem. And poor Wanda
appeared more than a little defensive. Did you see
how she yanked that silver cross up and down --
just the way she used to practically strangle
the life out of the bus cord when she'd
missed her stop -- remember?

Aunt Nell took it all pretty well, I thought,
except for the *kri'a**. She offered me
her sewing kit just before we started
in. But at least they could understand
the *dukhaning** -- Thank God they all knew
that one -- "May the Lord bless and keep you,
May the Lord make His face to shine upon you..."

Yes, it was a thing apart for most of them,
Mother, the *gemilut khesed** of this adopted faith.
But it doesn't matter, does it? Truly
It was for you, Mother.
It was for you.
*Aleha ha - Shalom**

**chazzan - the cantor who leads the Hebrew chanting of the service.*
tefellin - phylacteries. Two small black boxes containing handwritten verses from the Torah.
kri'a - a tear in the Jewish mourner's garment opposite the heart.
dukhaning -(Yiddish) - the priest's blessing.
gemilut khesed - deeds of loving kindness; acts done for the dead.
Aleha ha - Shalom - "Peace be upon her."

Wings

Lucilia Walker, R.N. worked third shift
in Charlotte, and soothed and rocked
and sang the babies she couldn't save
up into the arms of Jesus.

Be not dismayed, whatever betide. God will take care of you.
Beneath His wings of love abide. God will take care of you.

"Sure is hard sometimes, but these all God's
children. They'll be just fine."
Her charges, multi-hued and squalling,
seemed unconvinced.

God will take care of you.
Through every day, o'er all the way
He will take care of you.

Half truth at least. Not all the patients
died. Some left, went on to Little League
and Junior League, came back from schools
in Chapel Hill. As for the others, I
washed hands beside Nurse Walker and ignored
the empty isolette. Together we conspired
to find some purpose in another
mother's pain.

Through days of toil, when heart doth fail, God will take care of you.
When dangers fierce your path assail, God will take care of you.

Once at shift's close, a grateful father kissed her cheek,
offered sacks of summer beans and cherries.
Remembering childhood's farm, she smiled,
then rushed home to rest her legs
and raise four grandchildren
while her daughter worked.

Promptly at seven, the armies of hope marched in.
First shift's legions, men in coats white as milk
brought test results, launched crisp dispatches
on the progress of disease.
Later, four staff nurses, slender and serious
as cotton swabs, lent cool efficiency
to twilight's passing. Skilled hands started
I.V.s, tied sandbags to wrists to insure integrity
of tubes, while tiny fingers grasped
for flowers just out of reach.

God will take care of you.
Through every day, o'er all the way
He will take care of you.

Lucilia swooped in laughing at eleven.
Understaffed, behind again, she flew
among the bottles and the diapers,
the medicines and the unexpected
and eternal crises; and still she rocked
and sang, and somehow held them all,
even the one with eyes like mine, the boy
with one half kidney.

No matter what may be the test, God will take care of you.
Lean, weary one, upon His breast. God will take care of you.

My husband and I took turns with feedings,
napped on couches. The pattern seldom
varied. Each day I cried, shook tears
away and slept, then blessed in dreams
a large black bird with swollen feet, and prayed:
"Please, God, just let my baby live
'til third shift."

The Healing Art

for Ginger

You stand beneath the lights
serious as a surgeon,
your long fingers probing
deep within the chest
of yet another pie.

Hand firm on the pulse
of this kitchen, you listen
for signs: the whisper of siftings
from a blue bowl, the tip and lurch
of eggs across the counter, butter
throbbing on the stove. And on the sideboard,
awaiting your care, lie thin, depressed crusts,
pale, sinewy rhubarb and the little fevered cherries,
fat contemplative apples gazing up through
their lattice-work of sky, ever-swelling custards,
and the overwrought meringue.

The work of your heart goes out
in round glass pans, gladly given, and yet
there are days, surely, when you must feel
like Jesus -- "Lord, there are too many of them":
the children's neighbors, aunts, and the friends
of cousins, the bereaved and broken-spirited, hosts
and celebrants, hedonists who merely lust for lemon,
and the devout, who petition your offerings in order
to proclaim some personal epiphany of pumpkin.

Yours is a goodness deep as rivers,
and the closest I have ever come to God.
As you swim beneath the surface, through water
black as the eyes of berries, I can only watch
from a far shore, amazed and hungry for a faith
with kindness as its core. I would be always where
you are, and 'though I am sore unchurched and doubting,
still, I cannot imagine Heaven as a pieless place,
or any world without you in it.

III.
MOON PIE SOUTHERN GOTHIC

<<<<<<<<

Autumn Sonata

Spring abounds but fall abides.

i.

Always in the dragged out verdure of the season,
Almira Eberle imagined herself trapped within the pages
of a child's coloring book, imprisoned by an artist
with only one crayon. She resented spring
for its intensity, the pull and push, the urgent
agitation of it all. She was bored with the cow-eyed
antics of lovers and the cavortations of children,
and weary as God's seamstress
of the endless green.

Across most of her eighty-four years
Almira watched with amused detachment
through the time of tulips and tunafish
when people seemed caught like flocks of migrating
swallows in their odd, unthinking rituals. She marveled
at their energy -- those who wiped down
walls with sopping cloths, and crouched
with brooms to bully dustballs
from beneath the bed -- the ones who
gathered sticks and balls to swat
the day about -- and the truly religious
who knelt for months in damp black squares
praising with callused hands the fevered
fecundity of seed.

ii.

If spring was a dress that fit too tightly,
that pinched across the shoulders and bunched
about the waist, surely autumn was an old
sweater, loose and worn and soft, holding
in its every fiber the scented memory
of wood smoke and apple butter.

This was her time, the season that gave
everything it had, yet with grace
pulled back to let a body be.
She loved it all -- the weeks
when ripe pumpkins and late pansies
shared the garden, the nights of plaid flannel,
loved the pungent onion-garlic steep of rich
stews and the tang of cider, and loved
too, without really knowing why,
the whistle that called out those great
grunting giants to their games of pass
and pounce and pummel -- loved with abandon
their joyous lumbering gallopade
over white-lined fields
on Sunday afternoons.

iii.
Sometimes she wept this time of year
at the light, the paradoxical coolness of it,
the odd luminous angles, like once-upright
tomato vines now bent beneath
first frost.

She loved how the leaves put on
their brightest clothes to dance as they
died -- loved that any going could occasion
such celebration; loved too how the wind
sometimes took them back up after they'd fallen,
and how they flew then, free as bright tropical
birds whirling off to woods they'd never seen.
Even when they had lain for weeks brown
and drab as she-robins, Almira found them
beautiful, some of them spotted and stippled,
their faded edges curled up like shells,
listening. She loved them best perhaps
at the very last, when they had gone soft
and boneless clinging to moss and logs
and stones along woodland paths. She
loved then the grey-black smell of them
and their sound -- the sweet, wet suck
and slide of the earth pulling back
what was hers.

iv.

Almira loved autumn because it was prelude
to winter -- soft whispered answer
to a wish for solitude
and stillness, loved the fierce white
cold that covered everything, loved
that as far as you could run and everywhere
you looked, the world was blanketed
with silver and silence, and there was nowhere
anything
          green.

Massacre

Tenderly
I took them to the attic
and scalped them,
my beautiful dolls,
not out of anger,
rather from some impulse
I didn't understand,
vague restlessness
yearning
to be boy
or Indian.

Lone freckled girlchild,
huddled in the corner, hemmed in
by tablecloth and teacups,
surrounded
by porcelain face and fingertips,
gentle play and careful
kindnesses; I chose instead
to become warrior. Raging wild one
I carved out what was mine,
destroyed and changed it, slashing
away before me small hopes,
diminutive expectations,
as my younger sister, witness
to the carnage, wondered aloud
at possible implications
for motherhood.

I am a mother now and one day
I will tell my daughter,
"Strong princess brave
on a tall horse, be sure
of your heart. Take your large dreams
to the open prairies, and Daughter,
when you are cornered, never fear
to take in hand
what is yours
and cut
          deeply."

Talisman

What will they remember?
Not the call that comes at midmorning
nor the hiss of fear that slithers back
through the wires--not even the shock
of cold gel or the tug of electrodes
like eager mouths sucking for answers.

They will remember tears of rain
gathered at a window, dust motes floating
in a stream of hall light, voices that drift
down to them like feathers, and they will remember
the small secret things that saved them:
crumpled photographs and worn medallions,
the bright embroidered arms of worry dolls,
Stars of David and silver crosses, pebbled rosaries
and pockets of shells, and once, in the billow
of a pre-op paper slipper, a tiny yellow giraffe.

San Juan Capistrano, 1987

"They are grace, hope, thought on wings..."
-- John Burroughs

March 18th,
the mission courtyard colding
into evening. The figs' breath
rises, sour yet across the groves.
Lemons dream, hard within
their puckered skins, and roses
lean, sore and tight, against
the chapel gate. In the dust
only pigeons dance.

As sun nips the flank
of morning, herding lazy
clouds over purpling adobe,
the prodigals return.
The short grass stretches,
ferns unfurl in greeting.
They have come home,
our small, slim priests
in blue-black robes, twittering
prayers of blessing, working pellets
of mud like rosaries through their wide
shining beaks.

The Surgeon's Garden

The anger is a growing
thing, dark as the skin
of grapes or the underside

of violets, whose verdure
chokes me with reaching
tendrils and leaves

of fur and sorrow.
There was a time
when I could escape

this pounding pulse,
the pullulating pain
of this ripe hate's

unfolding; when laughter
called me, and the lure
of moonfoam, pale breath

of swallow flight, cloud
bruise and cicada song,
the soft white fringe

at the heart of the wolf's
mane. But no more. All
that I am is given

to rank gray foliage, sad
efflorescence of fear's
remembering; each day

the vetch grows longer,
taking from me life
as it expands; but I will

tend this plant until
its final burgeoning.
Only then can I return the gift

to him whose certain
callowness cut down my
husband, strong black

blooms for the man in green
with knives, who planted
the seed.

Hunter's Reel

after reading the poet's
apology to his namesake

A father and son should never
share a name;
a game of catch on Saturdays,
ties perhaps and aftershave, and maybe
in later years a friendly tea
on Sunday afternoons,
but not a name.
It is too much to ask.

But kids are easy,
and even though you violated that space
where the dreams of children
like small speckled eggs
lie nestled, waiting
to be born, he will forgive you,
and forget in time
that you bent his pride to your
purpose, demanded perfection when
desire could have sufficed, and mocked
as imitation his every pale echo
of your eloquence.

He will forgive you,
take your hand and hold you
with his eyes as together
you learn the steps
and count the measure
of this strange sad dance
of love and fear
between a father and a son.

Before the reel is done
you will change places:
he will claim the name
as you become the fleeting
quarry, smaller, more fragile
than when you began.

Too late the gesture
of appeasement and apology,
the lines that bare your neck
to him, and your heart;
for any poet's son knows
the secret: every poem is both
tribute and dismissal, warm word
quilt, edges all tucked in,
which covers over guilt
and allows us to sleep,
in sleep to dream of the open field
beyond the forest,
and the single stag,
standing in the center
of the clearing, still
and waiting, silent
easy prey.

The Garden

There are prayers to be spoken here.
Across the pond pulse the tongues of hummingbirds.

Smug zucchini lurks beneath muck and aspen gristle.
Some puddings are too thick for spoons.

Yellow wands of forsythia bend to bless kewpie-faced pansies.
Can too much be made of the wafer and wine?

I am caught up in the starched flamenco skirts of marigolds,
the vertigo of poppies.

Rain anoints pillows of snail slither.
A faint memory of light.

The scent of tweed resonates in new mown grass.
A quiver of small damp endings.

Spiders hang from the bones of azalea bushes.
How then shall we live?

Transformations

Hush daughter, it's all right.
My eyes can't see you well,
swathed as they are in wrappings
of mist and sea haze, but I don't mind
this softness of vision, brightness dulled
to the cool luminosity of dusk.
This I can abide.

When first my hands and feet
grew tinged with blue and cold,
I sought to remember the burnished
alabaster of Florence, smooth Carrara
marble. I tried to summon the quiet
at their core, the inexorable patience
of stone.

Later, when the fluids began to rise
again, and I sensed the swelling
coming on, I imagined a large purpling
grape -- thin impermeable walls stretching
to accommodate the water ripening
to sweetness within. I recalled
dusty origins in a vineyard by the sea,
the soft surge of seasons, endlessly shifting
currents of sugar and light.

And daughter, when I heard
that hard fluttering at my breast
and felt the first faint twitterings
of pain, I thought it was the redbirds
come back again, the sharp-beaked ones
whose small muscled backs and dripping
feathers bore you out into the world.

But I think that this dark bird
has come for me. Soon his broad
rake-wings will carve a path for us,
and we will fly out together, he and I,
laughing into brightest sunlight, screeching
down a clear road through tall rows
of perfect, budding corn.

Moon Pie Southern Gothic

I am purple woman
Georgia freckled lady
floating on the dancing river
word song, dream depth
of different lives embedded
in images that come
on late nights
and memories of mornings
down at the creek with B.J.,
toes dripping, log mind waiting
for deliverance of some important
news.

I am eternal daughter wife mother person
surrounded in every corner of my house
by good men seeking clean shirts
and mollybolts, Mars Bars for lunches,
a ride to the gym, a trip to the doctor,
but I am stronger than all
of these, my voice the echo
of wave pulse and seal whisper.
Beneath a creamsicle dusk
and bruised clouds, I stand shining--
shining like moonfoam
even as crabs circle.

I am every person
down the years whose sex and songs
and breath have made me, all those thousands
of genes and thoughts consorting
angrily lustily incongruously together.
I am my sister's stillborn son
with perfect fingers,

and I am the 130 year-old soldier
in blue who ran away. I am the diva
my father loved once, just as I am that shriveled
sunbonneted step-grandmother from hell
who hurt my mother and made us
wash our feet in toilets
to save the whiteness
of her towels.

I am red clay, open-mouthed grasshopper
laughter, lime pie lust, Coca-cola and Moon Pie
for breakfast. I am soft heavy azalea soul, rose
petals and sweating magnolias floating in a bowl, Christ
crucified in dogwood on Peachtree Street.

I am also the skunk cabbage, arid
sage root tumbleweed of this place, hurtling
over hay meadows, pulling the wind and the pine
and the snow cold
to me.

I am purple woman, and I want
to live forever in the sere, in the stone sure
love of the word, acorn coiled and budding
in that safe, sacred center of imagined space
where there is room for everyone
I have ever been
and will ever be.

Tide Pull

The last time I saw you, Grandfather, we shared a summer
of sandcrabs, flickerlight, and moonfoam,
bucket walks at midnight
and the pearl-grey skittering of cracked shells over toes.

You carried it with you then, great shifting dune
within your chest; but no one told me, rather deemed me
youngling too raw to recognize the shiver surge, tide pull
of mortality. Not that I would have believed them. Of all
the splotched and mottled elders and drab relations,
you were the young one, Grandfather, laughing gambler
with the golden voice and sandy hair. Surely you would be there
always to rescue my kites and right my boats and annihilate
my kings across the board.

Some mornings you slept late, lingered long in your deck chair
moored to green stripes, memorizing clouds, etching water's undulations
on your soul, searching billow and breaker for answer,
slowly rocking waves of bourbon in your glass.
You pulled up bloody phlegm in nets from your throat; squirming
red clams lay trapped in your handkerchief. I looked away then,
ran down to chase the gulls, to pull the stalks and crush
the shells of crabs.

We built castles in the last days, played more checkers,
tested the luck of the damned as we scratched lottery tickets
and lost, bet nickels on backyard contests of lizard and chameleon.
Once you knelt down to hold me in your eyes, and fingers redolent
of bluefish stroked my light brown hair.

There was no funeral.
Grandmother kept you in a box on her dresser, and you lay waiting
there, among lilac scents and bracelets of turquoise and coral,
all through winter and the green seasons, until an autumn later
when my mother and my aunt and grandmother--fierce huddled chorus
on a Piedmont flight to Hatteras--took you to the sea to let you out.

I had a dream, Grandfather.
I dreamed I saw you at the dancing edge of the ocean late
one evening--and it was you--not the bone-chunk death dust
they'd spoken of--but you, whole and handsome. I dreamed they left
you there, naked, at midnight, in a tide pool overlooked by cliffs
of sea oats and pampas grass. I called to you, but you could not
hear me. Your eyes looked unblinkingly up toward stars.
And you lay there in your tide pool, Grandfather,
illuminated by flickerlight and moonfoam, floating
forever floating
            forever hostage
                        to the crabs.

NOTES

Some of the biographical information in the poem "Suzanne Remembering", especially regarding artist Suzanne Valadon and particulars of her relationship with Eric Satie, was gleaned from the delightful book, *Lives of the Musicians*, by Kathleen Krull.

"Aerobic Valentine" was written after reading Stephen Dunn's magnificient twelve page poem "Loves," which appeared in POETRY, and in *Landscape at the End of the Century*, 1991, published by W.W. Norton and Company. The last line of my poem is a variation on Dunn's last line in "Loves".

The hymn, "God Will Take Care of You", which forms the chorus in the poem "Wings", was written by C.D. Martin and W. Stillman Martin, and appears in a number of texts, among them, *101 More Hymn Stories*, by Kenneth Osbeck, published by Kregel Publications of Grand Rapids, Michigan.

THANKS

Hillary Clinton has said that "It takes a village"to raise a child. Certainly, book rearing is only slightly less taxing. It, too, requires the love and considerable involvement of a small principality. I would like to thank the many individuals who helped to make this book possible:

Marilyn Wrucke, artist, friend and motivator, for her very visible work as photographer, for her enormous behind the scene labors, and especially for her love, respect and prodding.

My sister, *Suzanne Doten*, for her patience and for her herculean efforts on my behalf in typing, layout, and research. She will always be "part of the magic".

Donna Gallegos, Judy Miranda, and *Richard Watt* of Community College of Denver for their most necessary and invaluable assistance in the areas of layout, computer text flow, graphics and printing.

My editors, *Carolyn Campbell* and *Carolyn Wangaard*, for their belief in me, for their help and encouragement, and for their very essential support and endorsement through EVERGREEN WOMEN'S PRESS.

Ginger Black and *Margie Vogt* for the friendship that never falters, and the love that sustains me always.

My husband *Peter*, and our sons *Patrick* and *Brendan*, who always knew I could.

ABOUT THE AUTHOR

Donna Moyers Park was born in Knoxville, Tennessee, and grew up in Georgia. She attended Maryville College, and holds degrees from Memphis State University and the University of Denver. Her work has appeared in several magazines and anthologies, including *Kalliope* and *The Charlotte Poetry Review*. She lives with her husband, younger son, and two red dogs in Morrison, Colorado.

ABOUT THE ARTIST

Marilyn Closs Wrucke grew up on a farm in Fairmont, Minnesota and graduated from College of St. Benedicts in St. Joseph, Minnesota. She continues to experiment with all types of photography. Her work has most recently appeared in the Arvada Center for the Performing Arts publications. She lives with her husband in Morrison, Colorado and hikes with Donna (and Donna's two red dogs) in the foothills near their homes.